THE
GENTLE GIANTS

BY

ERNEST CLIFFORD HAZELL

AN ILLUSTRATED HISTORY OF A FAMILY OF
BRISTOL TIMBER HAULIERS 1880 - 1935

THE GENTLE GIANTS

Edited by

Ken Griffiths and Roy Gallop

Photographic Processing   John Brewer

Typography   Joanne Howard and Deborah Gough

Cover Design   Roy Gallop

Acknowledgements: Reproductions from 'Woodcuts by Thomas Bewick and his school.   Edited by Blanche Cirker. Published by Dover Publications Inc. New York 1962.
Our thanks to: Mildred Loring, the author's daughter, for access to original photographs, manuscripts, and material. Also for her patience in answering our endless questions; Joan Holley, the author's niece, for permission to use family photographs from her collection; Mr Mike Lowe, Editor, The Bristol Evening Post, for his permission to reproduce the letter from Mr Tucker.

PREFACE

In 1976 the Bristol Evening Post invited readers with experiences or memories of working Shire horses to record their recollections in writing. Letters received by the paper on this subject would be published and included in a competition. The winning letter was from Ernest Clifford Hazell, who received as his prize a copy of 'The Shire Horse' by Keith Chivers.

Four years later Mr Hazell ('Cliff', as he was known to family and friends) submitted a more comprehensive account of his recollections to the local history magazine 'Malago'. The article was published in 1980, and gives an insight into the workings of a timber haulage family business, using the Shire horse as motive power.

Cliff died in 1991, aged 83 years, but left behind an array of artefacts, writings and photographs in the safe hands of his daughter, Mildred. An examination of these reveals an interesting family history. The timber haulage business had its origins in the 1880s. Members of the Hazell family were still working with the 'Gentle Giants' until 1935, when they gave way to mechanised transport, which had been slowly developing since the First World War.

The central feature of this book will be Cliff's recollections contained in his original manuscript, which was the source material for the above-mentioned articles. Cliff's story will be complemented by photographs from the family collection. The book will also give a brief account of Cliff's personal and family history.

Cover: The author's father, James Hazell, with George Price and two teams of Shire Horses negotiating
a difficult slope on East Dundry Hill.
Title Page: The author's grandfather, Tom Hazell, photographed in 1882.

THE HAZELL FAMILY

Cliff's grandfather, Thomas Hazell started his timber haulage business in the early 1880s. Tom was born in Pensford, Somerset, in 1850. He did not undertake timber haulage as an occupation until his move to Bristol, where he resided until his death in 1911. He married Ann Cox, also of Pensford, and took up residence in Jarvis Street, Barton Hill, moving to a property in Meyrick Street at a later date. They had nine children.

One wonders how Tom acquired the skills to engage in a trade that required precision in it's processes, not least to ensure the safety of horses, operators, and the public. It must be understood of course that Tom would have grown up in a rural, labour intensive area. This would have brought him into close contact with people working in a variety of trades vital to an agricultural and mining community. The role of the Shire horse would have been of paramount importance in such an environment, and it is likely that Tom would have built up a fund of knowledge in both rural crafts and the handling of working Shires.

In any event by the early 1880s Tom was trading as a timber haulier, and was successful enough to eventually bring two of his sons, Sidney and Bertram, into the business. The business passed to Sid and Bert in 1911, trading under the name of Hazell Bros until they sold their City Haulage License to the Corporation in the 1930s.

Cliff's father James was born in 1876. He was the elder brother of Sid and Bert, and was also very much involved in timber haulage. He did not however work for the Hazell family. It appears that James was fostered by his Uncle Fredrick and Aunt Rosanna, Ann Cox's sister. Fredrick was a timber haulier and a modest property owner. He came to Bristol from Ebley, Gloucestershire. It is possible that his connection with the Hazell family through marriage may have been helpful to Tom during the early stages of his business.

Above: The author's grandmother, Ann, wearing a white dustcap, standing outside 41 Meyrick Street. Note the bricked up bay window next door. This house was used to stable the Shire horses

Facing Page: Tom Hazell with his wife and family at Jarvis Street. James, the author's father, stands behind him. Sidney is behind his mother, and Bert wears a sailor suit.

The fostering of Cliff's father by Fredrick and Rosanna may have been an informal affair. Nonetheless, Fredrick and Rosanna, who had no children, adopted a parental role in respect of James. On leaving school James commenced work for his uncle who traded under the name 'F. Niblett - Timber Haulier.'

James married Rose Davis in 1898 and moved to Parson Street, Bedminster in 1909, living in a dwelling built by Fredrick. Stables were built close by, and 'F. Niblett - Timber Haulier' was then able to work out of Bedminster, serving a large area of North Somerset. James worked as a horseman and timber man from 1885 until 1935. It must have seemed to James and his contemporaries in 1885 that horse working would always have a place in the social and economic life of the country. The impetus of the First World War however accelerated technological advances in a way never seen before, and it was inevitable that a mechanical replacement would be developed to supersede the working horse. Even so, their replacement was gradual, and Shires were still being used for heavy haulage and ploughing during the Second World War.

James and Rose had six children, and Cliff's brother Wilf followed his father into the business at the close of the First World War. Wilf was working for F. Niblett's when the business passed to his father, who became joint proprietor with Fredrick's nephew. Trading ceased in 1935. James retired and Wilf secured employment with Bristol City Council, where he remained until his retirement in 1968.

Rose, Cliff's mother, with baby Harry and Cliff centre, with younger brother, Stan, outside 46 Parson Street.

Unlike his brother, Cliff did not become a timber haulier. However, he did have close contact with many aspects of timber hauling during his formative years, and beyond. He built up a treasury of memories, some of which he relates in his article 'Shire Horses'.

Cliff's memories give a flavour of past times, and enrich our knowledge and understanding.

SHIRE HORSES
THE GENTLE GIANTS

by

Ernest Clifford Hazell

My memory of Shire Horses goes back to the time when one of a family of six children we lived at 46 Parson Street, Bedminster, in a cottage with an orchard and stables adjoining, where my great uncle, Fred Niblett kept 14 shires engaged in the business of Timber Hauling, hauling trees to the local timber yards. Horses were a family tradition, as two of my uncles also operated with two teams timber hauling from Barton Hill at about the same period, until sad to say the change over to modern transport.

The 14 made up 3 teams with 3 carriages, the drivers being my father, George Price, Bill Brown, and assisted by my brother Wilf, and young George Price. The journeys to the countryside varied in distance as the radius around Bristol stretched as far apart as Butcombe, Chelwood, Clevedon, Tockington and Bitton. This meant in those days a long day's work, remembering the walking the drivers had to do. Rain, sleet, snow and hard frost were all taken for granted.

No reins were used or needed for the horses' guidance as they were trained to obey by word of command, and addressed by name, each with a temperament of its own. Like children they sometimes needed to be corrected when slacking, hence the need of names. The drivers were well-known for miles around Bristol, and noted for their loud voices when shouting words of command.

I did not become a Timber Haulier myself, but remember the horses well by name. My job as a lad from about 1917 to 1922 was to clean out the stables, mix the chaff in the loft, fill the mangers, maybe fetch a horse from the blacksmiths in Fire Engine Hill that had been newly shod, or fetch some repaired harness from the saddlers. The nosebags and collars were nearly as tall as myself then. Time for playing was rather restricted.

One of the best sights I ever saw were 2 teams doubled up on one carriage to haul an extra large oak tree from Shirehampton Golf Course, coming up the steep hill out of Westbury-on-Trym. The tram driver behind, unable to pass, foolishly ringing his bell. Yes, even in those days some road users never had a minute to wait, or patience.

These horses were endowed with a wonderful brain as they had at times to obey the word of command at once. An instance of this would be rolling a tree up the skids on to the waggon when loading. Pulling too hard at the wrong time would turn the waggon over. It had to be rolled gently on to the top of the skid, and as soon as it reached the bed of the waggon, pulling had to stop at once. I never saw one tip over. The words of command were simple - "Gee Up" - go on, "Wont off" - go the right, "Come ee backway" - come left, and of course "Whoa" - stop.

It was also great to see a team with a full load going through the gateway of a field in the dead of winter, with mud and water up to the axles, horses going full pelt to keep the wheels turning, no room for drivers to walk by the side of the horses, and mud too deep anyway. They stood behind to shout instructions and crack their whips as a reminder that an all out effort was needed. The whip was seldom used on the horses. They knew what it was for though, as the cane used to be for us at school. The farmers had little to grumble at as their gates and posts were rarely damaged.

Another time when the brain of the shire was in strong evidence was hauling a heavy load up Battles Lane at Chew Magna. A double team had to be used, a build up of speed essential from the bottom of the steep hill right up to the tee junction at the top. There the sharp right hand turn had to be negotiated into the narrow High Street without damage to a stone wall in front, and those on either side. The overall length of the six trace horses in pairs, the shaft horse, timber waggon, and overlap of the tree at the back, was considerable. The waggon had to be swung around in one action with no stopping or damage to walls, so it meant the trace horses going over to the facing wall and hugging the side when swinging the load to the right. This was done with only inches to spare at the rear. What I remember so well were the shouts of command, the sparks from the horses shoes from the hard stone as it was then, and the all out effort of every horse against the collar. Battles Lane remains much as it was but the scene of that day is gone for ever.

The drivers were devoted to their horses, but it was very hard work and long hours of toil. Many times during a long wet winter men and horses would come home soaked into the lamp lit stables. Then it was off with the harnesses, and a quick rub down for each horse with a rough cloth to take off the worst of the sweat and rain. These tasks had to be completed before the days work could be called finished. A days work could sometimes be very long, a 6.00 am start and a 10.00 pm finish.

Starting out mornings to fetch the loads was a steady stroll as far as the horses were concerned, but coming back was at a much quicker pace. They did not require any bidding to get back to the warmth of the stables and a feed. They knew the roads home for miles around. Some horses, retired from hauling work were sold to farmers for lighter work on the farms, and would return to our stables on their own long after, from as far away as Butcombe or Stanton Drew, if a field gate had been left open. Mind you, the roads around Parson Street were a far cry from the rush and tear of today. On winter nights at home, it was a case of "Up to bed" for us children when the horses were heard coming home. We could hear the clomp of hooves and the rattle of chains from as far away as Fire Engine Hill. The full loads and waggons were quite often left at the saw mills for unloading in daylight the next day. I remember that the horses would race to the trough for a drink, with about four of them pushing to get their noses into their own stalls, and heads in the manger. If the harness was very wet on returning a big fire was built in the kitchen to dry the collars or loin cloths, if wanted for the morrow. The smell from the sweat and rain when the steam started to rise in the warm room was I suppose very unpleasant, and yet in a way was an experience very few people today will ever enjoy.

This is only a brief outline of what I know, but my brother Wilf could supply stories and photos of bygone days in a way I cannot, but like most good horsemen, he is too modest to write about his details of the runaway load on Rownham Hill, or the story of the farmers wife that stitched up a gash in the belly on one of our horses that got injured on a sharp branch of a tree. She used, as far as I can remember a needle and silk thread, with no ill effects to the horse. The gentle giants are a race apart, but their feet, with heavy shoes on come heavy, as I learned to my cost one day. Through my own fault I got stepped on by one. Whilst I expected some sympathy for the pain suffered, all I got was abuse from my father telling me that next time I would know the proper way to lead a horse out of the yard.

The past is gone for ever, but now those of our generation can enjoy the memories that others will never know. While I look back on those times as 'The Good Old Days', maybe my brother would not be in agreement. It was for him years of blood, sweat, tears, and toil, but he still looks at a good horse with pride, I know.

James, about 8 years of age, with his father Tom and Driver Dick Tracy. Tom's decorated stick was just a hedgerow stem carved with a knife and easily replaced.

Sid with the Barton Hill team outside 61 Redland Road, Bristol. Wilf, Cliff's elder brother, stands at the back of the timber carriage.

Outside the White Horse, West Street, Bedminster. Toogoods timber yard was just a short distance away.
The driver, Tom Reeves, emigrated to the USA before the First World War. (The horse was called John)

Tom Reeves, with loaded timber carriage waiting patiently to unload opposite Toogoods timber yard. Wintles shop was on the corner of West Street and Bartletts Road.

Cutting a tree prior to loading. James is supervising his son Wilf. The young helper in a cap lived in Highbury Road, Bedminster.

A tree being rolled up the 'skids' by the Shires (out of photograph to the right). Fredrick Niblett's name board can be made out on the back of the timber carriage.

Wilf standing on the tree trunk. Bill Brown, driver, and James pose for a photograph before the trace horses are hitched.

*'Boys will be boys'. Better than an adventure playground. Stan, Cliff's younger brother is holding Bonnie.
The Knowle Water Tower (on the horizon) was built in 1905, 12 years before this photograph was taken.*

The team at Cheltenham Road, Bristol. Wilf beside the shaft horse and father James at the rear. This photograph, taken in the 1930s, shows the increasing problem of mixing with mechanised traffic. Nevertheless the lead horse needs no guiding hand and appears calm and unconcerned.

Cliff's older brother, Wilf, outside the stables at 46 Parson Street. Bonnie was Wilf's favourite horse

"Glengarry",
1, Jubilee Road,
KNOWLE.

11th September, 1929.

Dear Sir,

I feel I must write and express my appreciation of a very kind and thoughtful act on the part of one of your men in charge of timber hauling wagon, to the horses.

On Friday night last two loads of timber came up Brislington Hill, and paused for rest after passing Talbot Road. One load had just passed on; the other was still resting. I was appreciating the man giving the horses a rest, but was wishing, so much that it could have been possible to have given them a drink, after that heavy pull up, at the water trough a few yards back. I realised it was impossible to stop the load at the trough, as the weight of timber would have been behind them on the hill, and also it is a dangerous corner in the dark. Judge of my gratified surprise therefore to see your man unharnessing all three horses, and taking them back for a drink. Doubtless your man was tired himself, but realised the horses had suffered more, and therefore put himself to the trouble of unharnessing in the dark. Perhaps the man in charge of other load had done the same, but, as I said before, he had passed on before I came. (It was about 9 p.m)

Would you please pass on the enclosed 1/- to the man in question, as a small appreciation of a kindness to animals from a working woman. Yours faithfully,

(Miss) M. Eisele

An unsolicited testimonial to the good care that the Hazell family took of their horses. The letter was sent to James, and it is believed that it was Wilf who was the person referred to by Miss Eisele.

The Gentle Giants, what an appropriate name for the Shires. How many other species of animals, or even humans, after a hard slogging day could find the energy and humour to give you a gentle nip with their teeth or send you flying with a hearty shove of their nose in the small of your back?

Being brought up a stones throw from Fred Niblett's yard, with his horses a familiar daily sight, I think Mr E.C. Hazell's letter illustrates the reason why the timber shire had the edge on the dray shire - their ability to move or deposit a heavy load at the right time and on the right spot.

As boys we watched them manoeuvre the loaded wagons into Toogoods yard (at that time opposite Bartletts Road where the garage now stands) and on several occasions after off-loading saw a team with the empty wagon move off driverless back to the stables over half a mile away to wait patiently outside for the uncoupling - reversing in the yard of the wagon ready for the morning and the bedding down for the night.

To those of us privileged to see a team of shires in action no internal combustion or jet engine will ever give the same thrill.

W. Tucker.
Bedminster, Bristol.

Copy of a letter sent to the Bristol Evening Post in 1976 in respect of the competition organised by Max Barnes.

THE BRISTOL JOCK
1908 - 1991

To those who never knew Cliff no greater insight into his character could be gained than to read his letters home to the family whilst on active service. They are informative, humorous, and in general uncomplaining, although sand, dust and flies figured largely in his dislikes. Cliff was destined for early fame, winning a baby contest in 1908. Rose, his mother, regarded this as a 'feather in her cap', as the show was organised by the C of E, and they were Methodists.

Cliff has written an account of his 'schooling' at Parson Street Primary. He used the word advisedly as he says it was certainly not education. It is an insightful, satirical account which clearly highlights the serious defects in the system at that time.

There was a great deal of interchange between the extended families in Bristol, Ebley, and the Chew Valley. Cliff did not follow his older brother, Wilf, into the family timber haulage business, but went to work in a market garden, owned by his aunt, Rose's sister at Ebley. His aunt has been described as a very dominant person and not to Cliff's liking, and although he was very keen on the work decided to return home after two years.

Work was hard to find in the twenties but Cliff got a job as a delivery boy with the Maypole Dairy Company in Central Bristol, but soon moved to their shop in Stokes Croft, where he worked his way up to be manager.

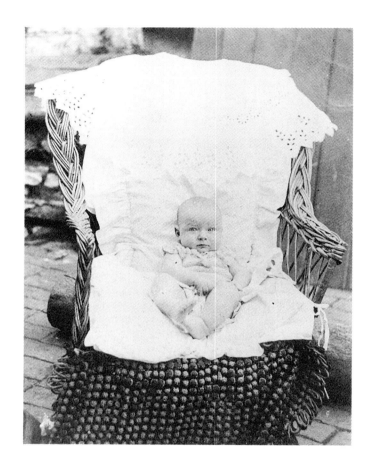

The author, about the time he won his first competition.

Cliff managed this shop in Stokes Croft, Bristol, before and after his army service. The shovel in the foreground has puzzled many people! Note the immaculate window display and prices.

By the late thirties Cliff, following a holiday romance, married Ada, who came from Manchester, and by the time he was called up in 1940, Mildred, their only child, had been born. He was 32 years of age when conscripted, old in comparison to his fellow squaddies and ironically, in time honoured fashion was nicknamed 'Junior'. This title followed him throughout his army career, which was remarkable in that he survived three separate campaigns.

On call up he was drafted into the Royal Signals, mainly because of his motorcycling ability, and became a despatch rider attached to the 51st Highland Division with which he served throughout the Second World War.

Facing Page: A group of despatch riders, the photograph probably taken in Scotland before embarkation to Egypt via the Cape. Cliff is standing behind the right handlebar of the motorcycle.

Above: A not so 'Gentle Giant'. Cliff often commented on the dust that they had to ride through in the desert.

Cliff was in the Western Desert with the Eighth Army, the landings at Salerno, and the subsequent battle for Italy, and then Northern Europe following D-Day. He contracted malaria in Sicily and had a further recurrence in Holland in 1944. As a despatch rider he commuted between the many Scottish Regiments that made up the 51st Highland Division. He was famed for his Bristol/Jock accent. Communications between Cliff and the Glaswegian Scots of the Black Watch must have relied heavily on hand signals.

On demobilisation Cliff returned to Bristol and the Maypole but was soon asked to take over one of their shops in what was then a 'difficult' part of the city. After a very trying start Cliff with his good humour and no nonsense approach made a great success of the store.

Rabbits, pigeons, and his garden had always been important to Cliff, and following Ada's death in 1960, and his retirement in 1973 he became more involved in these interests.

Cliff's older brother Wilf was reticent about his work with horses, and when in the Seventies and Eighties there was a renewed and growing interest in Shires Cliff was able to relate not only his own experiences as a boy, but to record Wilf's account of the Hazell family's day to day work with the Gentle Giants.

Facing Page: Cliff with Ada and Mildred at Lewis Road, Bedminster Down. This picture was taken towards the end of the war. Note the 'Balmoral' worn by members of the 51st Highland Division.

Other titles by FIDUCIA PRESS include

The Organ Grinder by T.R. Lamb (A verbal obsession) £3.00

Fussells Ironworks - Mells (A History of the Ironworks, the Family and the
Community) by K. Griffiths and R. Gallop £2.00

Tracts from the Tracks. Collected Poems by Mark Griffiths £2.00

Published by Fiducia Press,c/o 35 Stackpool Road, Southville, Bristol, BS3 1NG.
Copyright Ken Griffiths and Roy Gallop. Photographs are from the Hazell family collection. All
rights reserved; no part of this book may be reproduced, or transmitted in any other form or by
means, electronic or mechanical including photocopying, recording or by any information,
storage, retrieval system, without written permission of the publishers.